"Teacher Bob," said Ferdy, "you'll be pleased to hear that my teammate and I have finally agreed on an invention."

"Glad to hear it," said Bob. "How did you manage to agree?"

"I've been doing some reading on conflict resolution," said Ferdy. "I used one of the ideas I'd read about."

"Yeah," said Too-Tall. "I always thought conflict resolution meant a punch in the nose."

"The idea was that it's sometimes better to write things down than to shout at each other," continued Ferdy. "So that's what we did. We each made a list of five inventions. Our hope was that at least one invention would be on both lists—and it worked! One invention *was* on both lists."

When Teacher Bob read the lists, his heart sank. The invention that appeared on both lists was…GUNS!

BIG CHAPTER BOOKS

The Berenstain Bears
NO GUNS ALLOWED

by the Berenstains

A BIG CHAPTER BOOK™

Random House New York

Copyright © 2000 by Berenstain Enterprises, Inc.
All rights reserved under International and Pan-American Copyright Conventions. Published in the United States by Random House, Inc., New York, and simultaneously in Canada by Random House of Canada Limited, Toronto.

www.randomhouse.com/kids
www.berenstainbears.com

Library of Congress Cataloging-in-Publication Data
Berenstain, Stan, 1923–
The Berenstain Bears: no guns allowed / by Stan & Jan Berenstain.
    p. cm. — (A big chapter book)
SUMMARY: When an increase in rudeness and aggressive behavior is noticed at Bear Country School, teachers and parents decide that something must be done.
ISBN 0-679-88953-1 (trade). — ISBN 0-679-98953-6 (lib. bdg.)
[1. Bears—Fiction.   2. Schools—Fiction   3. Firearms—Fiction
4. Violence—Fiction]   I. Berenstain, Jan, 1923–   . II. Title.
III. Series: Berenstain, Stan, 1923–   . Big chapter book.
PZ7.B4483Beah   2000   [Fic]—dc21   99-047879

Printed in the United States of America March 2000 10 9 8 7 6 5 4 3 2 1

BIG CHAPTER BOOKS is a trademark of Berenstain Enterprises, Inc.
RANDOM HOUSE and colophon are registered trademarks of Random House, Inc.

Contents

Chapter 1
The Culture of Violence

More and more sounds like *"Bang! Bang! You're dead!"*, *"Rat-a-tat-tat!"*, and "Take that, you no-good rat!" were being heard in the schoolyard of Bear Country School.

They were the sounds of pretend shoot-'em-up gunplay, and they were worrying Mr. Honeycomb, the school principal. So much so that he called a special early-morning teachers' meeting to discuss what he saw as a growing problem.

"What problem is that, chief?" asked Mr. Grizzmeyer, assistant principal and coach of the school's athletic teams.

"The growing problem of the culture of violence, and not just here at school, but in Bear Country generally," said Mr. Honeycomb.

"Huh?" said Mr. Grizzmeyer.

"I think what the chief is referring to," said Teacher Bob, who was Brother Bear's teacher, "is the changing atmosphere here in Bear Country—the growing rudeness, the pushing and shoving, the threats and name-calling."

"Hmm," said Mr. Grizzmeyer, growing thoughtful, which was unusual for Mr. Grizzmeyer. He was more a bear of action than a bear of thought. "I think I know what you're talking about. I've noticed a change even on the athletic field. Of course, there's

HUH?

MR. HONEYCOMB

a certain amount of conflict built into sports like football and wrestling. But there's a lot more trash-talking and name-calling lately—even in practice. Why, just yesterday, Milton Chubb and Too-Tall got into a nasty name-calling match during wrestling practice. They almost came to blows. I couldn't understand it. I expect that sort of thing from Too-Tall, but not from Milton."

The others nodded in agreement. They'd all had their share of problems with Too-Tall and his gang of ruffians.

"But Ferdy—he's team manager— explained that Milton's been watching something called *Grapplemania*. It seems to have changed Milton's whole personality. So I took a look at it. It's not even real wrestling, it's show wrestling with a lot of pumped-up monsters yelling and screaming and name-calling."

"I've seen it," said Teacher Bob. "I don't think it's harmful to all cubs, but it can be bad for some cubs—like Milton, for instance."

"Exactly," said Mr. Honeycomb. "That's another problem with the culture of violence. It's contagious, like measles."

"We could just make a school rule: no trash-talking or shoot-'em-up games on the school premises," suggested Mr. Grizzmeyer.

"We could," said Mr. Honeycomb. "But I don't think it would stick. Besides, we'd just be dealing with the symptoms, not the causes."

"Maybe," said Miss Glitch, who was the

school's reading specialist, "we should remove all violent literature from the library."

"Maybe," said Teacher Bob, "but that would mean getting rid of such great authors as William Shakesbear and Robert Grizzly Stevenson. I don't think you'd want to do that."

Miss Glitch agreed that she didn't.

"I agree with Mr. Grizzmeyer," said Teacher Jane, who taught the younger cubs, including Sister Bear. "It's also no longer just the boys. Now the girls—even the younger ones—are playing these '*Bang-bang!* You're dead!' games."

"I think we have to get down to basics," said Mr. Honeycomb. "What's the cause of the problem? Well, I don't think there's any doubt about the cause. *Grapplemania* may be a part of it, but it's *all* the violent television, violent movies, and violent video games. Why, it's guns, guns, guns, shoot, shoot, shoot, wherever you look. It's bound to influence our cubs. It goes far beyond the schools, but as educators, I think it's our responsibility to try to do something about it."

"Like what?" asked Mr. Grizzmeyer.

"I'm open to any and all suggestions, but here's what I propose: since it's a community problem, let's invite the community to a meeting right here at school to discuss it— the parents, the cubs, the community lead-

ers. Everybody will be welcome. If you think it's a good idea, we can send a notice home today."

"It's okay with me," said Mr. Grizzmeyer.

"I'll go along," said Miss Glitch.

"It certainly can't hurt," said Teacher Jane.

"I think it's a good idea, too," said Teacher Bob. "But there's another angle I'd like to explore. I agree with you about the culture of violence. But there's something going on right here at Bear Country School that's making a bad situation worse. It's the culture of cliques. I've been working on an idea about how to break down that culture."

"Culture of cliques?" said Mr. Honeycomb. "Cliques *are* a problem. What do you have in mind?"

"Well," said Teacher Bob, "here's what I'm planning to do…"

CLIQUE # 1

CLIQUE # 3

CLIQUE #2

E=MC²

CLIQUE # 4

CLIQUE #5

Chapter 2
The Culture of Cliques

Even as Teacher Bob spoke, the culture of cliques was in full operation in the schoolyard of Bear Country School. But there are cliques and there are cliques.

Some cliques, like Brother Bear's group—which consisted of himself, Bonnie Brown, Cousin Fred, and the younger tagalongs, Sister Bear and her friend Lizzy Bruin—were just a group of cubs who liked each other and got along.

Another group, the one that consisted of super-smart Ferdy Factual, Trudy Brunowitz, and Harry McGill, was based on its members' genius-level IQs.

There was also a girl group, which included Queenie McBear, Babs Bruno, and Bertha Broom. Though they had very different interests, they had one interest in common: they were strong feminists.

And there was a geek group, made up of would-be comedian Barry Bruin; his best friend, Gil Grizzwold; and anybody else they could rope in.

And, of course, the notorious Too-Tall Gang was a group unto itself.

Unfortunately, however, the Too-Tall Gang didn't *keep* to itself. They wandered around, accidentally-on-purpose bumping into other groups. This gave them the perfect opportunity to tease, taunt, threaten, and otherwise torment all the other groups in the schoolyard.

"Hey, Ferdy," said Too-Tall, brushing past the smaller cub. "There's a program about nuclear physics on cable TV tonight."

Ferdy gave him a puzzled look. "How in the world did you find that out?" he asked.

"A little *nerdy* told me!" said Too-Tall. He joined gang members Skuzz, Vinnie, and Smirk in raucous laughter.

"Hey, Barry," said Too-Tall as the gang wandered on. "I got one for you. Why did the chicken cross the road?"

"That's too easy, big guy," scoffed Barry. "To get to the other side, of course."

"Wrong, riddle breath," said Too-Tall. "The answer is: *to get away from your lousy jokes!*"

But the Too-Tall Gang did more than tease and taunt. They were not above more serious offenses. Sometimes they would surround a younger cub, stick a finger in his back as if it were a gun, and demand money.

But the worst trouble they'd gotten into was during recess one day when Teacher Bob happened to be on yard duty. Bob made it a practice to try to keep an eye on troublemakers (otherwise known as the Too-Tall Gang). When he couldn't locate them in any of their usual spots, he began scanning the horizon. And there they were, outside the fence, pointing what looked like guns into the schoolyard.

Teacher Bob ran to the fence as fast as

he could, jumped over it, and came up behind the gang, who were aiming and going, *"Pow! Pow! Pow! Pow!"* Of course, the guns weren't real. They were broken-off tree branches. But they looked a lot like guns.

Teacher Bob was very angry. Too-Tall and the gang had never seen him so angry.

"What in the world do you think you are doing?" he shouted at the top of his lungs.

The gang couldn't figure out what Bob was so excited about.

"Gee whiz, Teach," said Too-Tall, "we're just playing *Firing Squad.*"

"FIRING SQUAD?" screamed Bob.

"Yeah, *Firing Squad,* the hot new video game. It's fabulous. Here's how it works. You see, you're the firing squad and…"

"Give me those guns—er, branches—and get back over the fence into the

schoolyard!" said Teacher Bob.

Too-Tall and the gang discussed Bob's reaction as they moved back into the schoolyard. Bob overheard what they said.

"What do you think Teacher Bob was so mad about?" asked Skuzz, who was Too-Tall's chief lieutenant.

Too-Tall shrugged. "Beats me," he said. "Maybe he was mad because we went outside the schoolyard during recess."

Teacher Bob sighed. He didn't report Too-Tall and the gang for going outside the schoolyard, but he did tell Mr. Honeycomb about the "guns." It was one of the things that got the principal thinking about the culture of violence.

Chapter 3
No More Mr. Nice Guy

Teacher Bob was a very popular teacher. One of the reasons he was so popular was that unlike Miss Glitch, who was very strict and had rules for everything, he allowed his students a certain amount of freedom. While Miss Glitch had a "complete silence in class" rule, Teacher Bob allowed student-to-student conversation as long as it was about classroom work. He even allowed would-be stand-up comic Barry Bruin to tell a joke at the beginning of each day. It was called the "Joke of the Day," though Barry's classmates called it the "Groaner of the Day."

"The Joke of the Day," said Barry, standing up.

"Sit down, Barry," said Teacher Bob.

"Who ever heard of a sit-down comic?" grumped Barry, sitting down. "Anyway, the Joke of the Day: What did the preacher say to the skunk?"

"We don't know," droned the class in unison. "What *did* the preacher say to the skunk?"

"You've got the right church, *but the wrong pew!*" said Barry, standing up and taking quick little bows.

The class groaned in unison.

"Okay, class. Let's settle down," said Teacher Bob. "Here's the story for the day. I've got some bad news, some good news, and some bad news."

The members of the class looked at each other and wondered what was up.

"The first bit of bad news," said Bob, "is that you're all going back to the seats that were assigned to you at the beginning of the school year."

The class cried out in dismay.

"How come?"

"Oh, no!"

"No fair!"

One of the things Bob felt he'd been too easygoing about was classroom seating. He had assigned seats at the beginning of the year, but as time passed, he allowed his students to drift into seats of their own choosing. Thus it was that Brother Bear had

HOW COME?   NO FAIR!   OH, NO!

moved to the seat next to Bonnie Brown. Ferdy and Trudy had moved to aisle seats so they could team up with fellow brain Harry McGill, who was in a wheelchair. Where Too-Tall's seat was depended on whether his on-again, off-again relationship with Queenie was on or off. If it was on, he sat next to Queenie. If it was off, he sat in Spitball Corner with his gang.

The problem, as Bob saw it, was that the class was no longer a class. It was more like a group of warring islands constantly sniping at each other. Forcing his students to move back to their assigned seats was just the first step in his plan to do something about the clique problem.

Too-Tall was the one who made the most noise about having to sit where he was told.

"Gee whiz, Teach, you can't do this! What's the big deal about where we sit?

If I can't sit near my sweetie, Queenie, I won't be able to learn."

Milton Chubb, who was something of a loner and the only one who was still sitting in his assigned seat, stood up.

Good grief, thought Teacher Bob. Milton was wearing a *Grapplemania* shirt. That's what Mr. Grizzmeyer had been talking about that very morning. The shirt showed a big fist holding a bolt of lightning.

"Too-Tall, why don't you shut up and do what you're told," said Milton in a strong voice. And speaking of strong, though Milton was on the heavy side—it was not for nothing that he was called Massive Milton—powerful muscles were hiding under all that baby fat. He was, in fact, the wrestling champ of Bear Country School. He had achieved that rank soon after moving into the Beartown neighborhood with his mom and dad, who were hired bears on Farmer Ben's farm.

The class was shocked to see normally quiet and shy Milton challenging Too-Tall. Too-Tall was a little shocked himself. He just sat there and stared at Massive Milton.

"Didn't you hear me, moron?" said Milton. "Just shut your mouth and do what Teacher Bob told you!"

"Oh, yeah?" said Too-Tall, getting over his shock. "Who's gonna make me?"

"*I'm* gonna make you—me, myself, and I!" said Massive Milton. The class immediately took sides, making things worse.

"Tear 'em to pieces, Milton!" shouted Trudy. Teacher Bob had never heard Trudy speak a harsh word before.

"Squash 'em like a bug!" urged Ferdy.

Even Cousin Fred, who was a most peaceable cub, added to the atmosphere of violence. "Rip 'em to pieces!" he shouted.

The only ones on Too-Tall's side were his gang and Queenie. "Go get 'em, big guy! Pop 'em! Eat 'em alive!" shouted Queenie.

Teacher Jane was right, thought Bob. *It*

isn't only the boys that have gotten caught up in the culture of violence.

"ALL RIGHT! THAT WILL BE ENOUGH!" shouted Teacher Bob, bringing the flat of his hand down on his desk with a loud *wham!* "Milton, you sit down immediately, and the rest of you, move to your proper seats!"

"Yes, sir," said Milton.

The rest of the class moved to their proper seats.

Bob took some deep breaths to calm down. Mr. Honeycomb was right. The name-calling and the threats were getting out of hand.

"Excuse me, Teacher Bob."

It was Miss Glitch, leaning in the classroom door. "I have these notices to be sent home with the students."

Bob thanked Miss Glitch and looked at

the notice that was on top of the stack she had given him. This is what it looked like:

COME ONE! COME ALL!
TO AN IMPORTANT MEETING
Subject:
The Growing Culture
of Violence in Bear Country
Be it proposed:
Television, movies, video games, and gun violence are having
a negative effect on our cubs.
The Time: Tonight at 8:00 P.M.
The Place: The auditorium
at Bear Country School.
Come join in this
important discussion!
Speakers will include
Mayor Horace J. Honeypot and
Chief of Police Bruno.
BE THERE!!!!

Bob put the notices aside and pretended to mark papers until he had calmed down. He noted out of the corner of his eye that Too-Tall had his hand up. After letting Too-Tall stew for a while, Bob said, "Yes?"

"Well," said Too-Tall, "it's just that a little while ago, you said there was gonna be some good news."

"After that performance you all just put on," said Bob, "I'm not sure you deserve any good news." The class looked so crest-fallen he took pity on them.

"The good news," he explained, "has to do with our next major study unit." He walked up to the blackboard and chalked the word INVENTIONS in big letters.

"Hey, great!" said Harry McGill.

"Terrific!" said Brother Bear.

"I can live with that," said Queenie.

"Excuse me, sir," said Ferdy, "but inventions is a rather broad category, ranging from the wheel, which was invented at some unknown early time, up to the rather recent explosion of inventions in the field of electronics."

"Whadhesay? Whadhesay?" mocked Too-Tall.

"It's a perfectly good point," said Teacher Bob. "Here's what's going to happen. Of course, I'm going to have to sign off on them, but you're all going to choose your own inventions. You're going to do your own research. Then you're going to present your invention to the class. You're going to tell about its importance, its place in history, how it's benefited bearkind—that sort of thing. And I'm telling you right now, I'm expecting some fine presentations."

Even Too-Tall was excited about the inventions project. "I've got my invention!"

he cried. "The flush toilet!"

"The flush toilet?" said Babs Bruno. "Why don't you get your mind out of the gutter?"

"My mind's not in the gutter," protested Too-Tall, "it's in the—"

"Never mind, Too-Tall," said Teacher Bob.

"Hey, wait a minute. I'm serious," said Too-Tall. "Is the flush toilet an important invention or isn't it?"

Bob turned to Ferdy Factual. "How would you answer Too-Tall's question, Ferdy?"

"It's certainly not an invention I would choose," said Ferdy. "It's just not very interesting from a technical point of view. But it appears to pass the test: it's historically important and it certainly has benefited bearkind."

"Way to go, little fella!" said Too-Tall, reaching across and offering his hand for a high five. Surprised, Ferdy accepted the offer. It was the first exchange he'd had with Too-Tall that wasn't an insult. Bob was pleased.

The class was buzzing with excitement about inventions. Bob heard many inventions being mentioned: television, radio, the airplane, moving pictures. The class was still abuzz when Brother raised his hand.

"Yes?" said Teacher Bob.

"At the start of class, you said you had some bad news, some good news, and some bad news. Doesn't that mean we've still got some bad news coming?"

"That's right," said Bob. "And here it is: this is going to be a team project; you're all going to work in teams."

"What's bad about that?" asked Brother.

"We've worked in teams lots of times. I always work with Bonnie."

"That's right," said Too-Tall. "And I always work with my gang."

"And, of course, I always work with Trudy and Harry," said Ferdy.

"But not this time," said Teacher Bob. "This time, *I'm* going to pick the teams." The members of the class looked at Teacher Bob in stunned silence. "And I don't want any complaints," said Bob. "I am going to assign the teams tomorrow. Meanwhile, I want you to think about which invention you're going to choose. Now let's move on. We have other things to cover. But before we do, I want to hand out these notices. You're to take them home to your parents."

The cubs were so upset that they hardly looked at the notices before sliding them into their loose-leaf binders.

Chapter 4
Bang-Bang! You're Dead!

Since Brother and Sister Bear were a couple years apart, they had different ideas about what was fun. Though Sister was a strong and lively cub (she was a great rope jumper; once she had reached a thousand), what she enjoyed most was playing with her dolls and stuffed toys. Her idea of a really fun thing to do was to have a tea party for them.

Brother, on the other hand, wanted no part of tea parties for dolls and stuffed toys. Brother's idea of fun was playing step ball or practicing soccer moves.

"I wish they could find some way to play together," their mother would say on days when Lizzy and Cousin Fred couldn't come over and Brother and Sister would complain that they had nobody to play with.

There's an old saying that goes, "Be careful what you wish for, because you might get your wish." That's what happened with Mama's wish.

Brother and Sister did find a game they could play together. It had different names. Sometimes it was called "Good Guys Versus Bad Guys." Sometimes it was called "Cops and Robbers." Sometimes it was called "Space Bandits Versus the Interplanetary Police." But whatever it was called, it sounded the same. It was *"Pow-pow-pow! Bang-bang!* You're dead!" from when they got home from school until supper. It was really getting on Mama's nerves.

To make matters worse, after supper and homework they would watch "*Bang-bang! You're dead!*" television until bedtime, with perhaps a little time out for some "*Bang-bang! You're dead!*" video games. And what made matters even worse, Mama was very nervous about guns.

"Oh, dear!" Mama would say when she heard the *blam-blam* of neighbor Farmer Ben's shotgun. "I wish Farmer Ben wouldn't do that."

"What do you want him to do?" asked Papa. "Varmints are killing his chickens."

"I know," said Mama with a sigh. "It's just that guns worry me so. I really don't

BANG-BANG! YOU'RE DEAD!

understand why Brother and Sister are so devoted to these gun games. Why, I never even allowed them to have toy guns."

"Sweetie," said Papa, "I don't think it's anything to worry about. After all, I used to go to shoot-'em-up movies every Saturday when I was a cub, and it hasn't hurt me."

"Yes, but it's different now," said Mama. "Now it's *bang-bang*, you're dead, seven days a week." *Blam-blam* went Farmer Ben's shotgun off in the distance. "Oh, dear," said Mama. "I wish he wouldn't do that."

"But, sweetie," said Papa, "he's got to protect his chickens."

Mama just sighed and went into the kitchen to begin preparing supper. Papa shrugged. He had some work to do in his shop. He headed out the door and down the front steps. Unfortunately, the cubs had piled some cordwood on the steps as part of their game.

"I-I-I-I-E-E-E-E!" cried Papa as he took a header down the front steps. The cubs ran to where Papa was piled up at the bottom.

"Papa! Papa! Are you hurt?" they cried.

"Not seriously," said Papa. "But I have a question: DON'T YOU KNOW ANY GAMES BESIDES THESE INFERNAL 'BANG-BANG! YOU'RE DEAD!' GAMES?"

"Gee whiz, Papa," said Brother, "it's only pretend."

Later, during supper, Mama said, "I was talking with Mrs. Bruin. She says she's having the same problem with Lizzy and Barry. She says the problem is the growing culture of violence here in Bear Country."

The phrase "culture of violence" rang a bell with Brother. He'd just seen it. But

I-I-I-I-E-E-E-E!

where? Then he remembered.

"Excuse me, please." He hopped out of his chair and went to his book bag, pulled out the notice, and gave it to Mama.

"I do declare," said Mama as she read the notice. "There's a big meeting tonight on this very subject." She handed it to Papa. "If we hurry, we can finish our supper and clean up in time to get over to school for the meeting."

Chapter 5
Come One! Come All!

Mr. Honeycomb's notice must have touched a nerve among the bears of Beartown, because the school auditorium was filled to overflowing.

The crowd consisted mostly of parents of cubs from Bear Country School. Brother and Sister's grandparents had heard about it; they came to the meeting, too. The members of the Bear family took up most of one row. Many of those present were from Brother's class.

Word of the meeting must have spread far and wide, because it wasn't just parents that came to the meeting. Farmer and Mrs. Ben were there, as was Dr. Gert Grizzly, Beartown's leading physician and the director of Beartown Hospital.

The meeting even brought out old Mose Moseby, the whiskery old hermit who lived in a shack at the edge of Forbidden Bog. Old Mose was somebody few of those present had ever seen. There was even a reporter from the *Beartown Intelligencer*.

Up onstage were Mr. Honeycomb, principal of Bear Country School; Chief of

Police Bruno; and Horace J. Honeypot, mayor of Beartown. Mr. Honeycomb came to the rostrum and tapped the microphone to see if the loudspeaker system was working. *Klunk! Klunk! Klunk!* It was working.

"First," said Mr. Honeycomb, "I want to thank you all for being here. I want to get right down to business and say why we have called this meeting. For the benefit of those who may not have received the notice inviting you to this meeting, let me direct your attention to this blow-up."

He pointed to the blow-up. Using a pointer, he read aloud from the notice: "Subject: The Growing Culture of Violence in Bear Country." He turned to the audience. "How do we know about that? We

SUBJECT
THE GROWING
CULTURE OF
VIOLENCE IN
BEAR COUNTRY

know about it because we have seen the steady growth of rudeness, threats, name-calling, and violent play among the cubs of Bear Country School. Now here's the important part."

He took up the pointer again and read from the blow-up. "Be it proposed: Television, movies, video games, and gun violence are having a negative effect on our cubs." Again to the audience: "That's what we are here to discuss, but first, Chief of Police Bruno has a few words on the subject." The chief came to the microphone.

"Thank you, Mr. Honeycomb," said the chief. "First I want to say that I'm not some kind of psychologist or expert. I'm just a cop. But as a member of the police force and a father as well—my daughter, Babs, goes to school here—I'm taking this culture of violence thing very seriously. Especially the matter of gun safety. There've already been a couple of cases in Big Bear City where cubs have brought guns to school—real live loaded guns."

"Oh, dear!" said Mama, who found guns very worrisome.

"Some of you might say," continued the chief, "'That's Big Bear City. It can't happen here.' What I say is that it's better to be safe than sorry. Now a word from our mayor, the Honorable Horace J. Honeypot."

"Uh-oh," said Gramps, turning to Brother, "here comes old Mugwump."

The Honorable Horace J. Honeypot, who had a way of getting the fronts and backs of his words mixed up, came to the microphone.

"I can't tell you how pleased I am to he beer—er, be here. Like everything else, this pun groblem—er, gun problem—has soo

tides—er, two sides. And as your mayor, I just want to say I agree with both of them. Now I return you to Mr. Coneyhomb—er, Mr. Honeycomb."

"What's a mugwump, Gramps?" asked Brother Bear.

"It's a politician who sits on the fence with his mug on one side and his wump on the other," said Gramps.

"Thank you, Mr. Mayor," said Mr. Honeycomb. "Now let's start the discussion. The floor is open for any and all comments and questions." A number of hands shot up. "Yes, ma'am," said Mr. Honeycomb, pointing to Mrs. Bruin, mother of Lizzy and Barry.

"I just want to say that I agree with everything you and the chief said—especially the part about guns. I think guns are awful! I don't know why folks have to have them!"

"Right on!" said Mama, standing up and thrusting her fist in the air. Papa and the other members of the Bear family looked at the normally shy Mama with some surprise. Nor was Mama's the only voice raised against guns. Many mothers in the audience agreed.

"And furthermore—" continued Mrs. Bruin.

"I demand the right to be heard!" It was Farmer Ben. He was red-faced with anger.

"Not until I'm finished!" said Mrs. Bruin. "So sit down and shut up!" It was beginning to look as if the culture of violence might be coming to the meeting about the culture of violence.

"Please, Farmer Ben!" said Mr. Honeycomb. "I'm sure we all want to hear what you have to say. Now if you'll just allow Mrs. Bruin to finish…"

"And furthermore," repeated Mrs. Bruin, "I'm stopping all violent television and movies and video games at my house! And I urge all other parents to do the same!"

The sound of booing was heard in the audience. It was the cubs protesting.

Oh, dear, thought Mr. Honeycomb. *This is getting out of control.*

Farmer Ben was pumping his hand to be heard.

"Er, yes, Farmer Ben?"

Farmer Ben stood up. He looked like a storm cloud. "I just want to say that it makes no nevermind to me what you do about television, movies, or video games. Don't watch it. Don't go to 'em. Don't play 'em. But don't mess with my shotgun! Not unless you want to come over and protect my chickens from varmints!"

Now the audience was abuzz. Little arguments were breaking out all over—and they were getting bigger.

"Please!" said Mr. Honeycomb. "I must ask you to remain calm. We're all friends here, and..."

Another voice cut through the din. "Friends, you say! Well, yer no friends of mine!" It was Mose Moseby, the whiskery old hermit who lived at the edge of Forbidden Bog. "I say yer a bunch o' nosy busybodies stickin' yer nose into what ain't none o' yer business! As fer guns—I got thirty-seven of 'em. And I'm gonna keep 'em. It's a bear's natural-born right to bear arms. And if we get invaded by some of them Martians, don't come runnin' to me fer per-tection! Now if you'll excuse me, I'm goin' home and mind my own business!"

"Er, I assure you, Mr. Moseby, nobody wants to take away your guns," said Mr. Honeycomb. But Mr. Moseby had already stomped out of the auditorium. The audi-ence had gone quiet. Mr. Moseby's speech

had convinced them that the differences among the rest of the audience weren't as great as they seemed.

Mr. Honeycomb moved on with the meeting. "My staff and I have prepared a little presentation. We have taken bits and pieces of television, movies, and video games and made a film to show you. Our thought is that with parents as busy as you are, some of you may not know the kind of violence your cubs are watching. The screen, please."

Gus, the school's bear-of-all-work, pushed a movie-type screen onto the stage.

"All right, Bob, start the film!" said Mr. Honeycomb.

The lights went down, and Teacher Bob, who was in charge of the projector, started the film. It included bits of television shows, movies, and video games such as *Grapplemania, Big Bear City Blue, Lethal Gun, Natural Born Killer-Dillers, Firing Squad,* and *Here's Blood in Your Eye.*

The film wasn't very long, but it had more violence in it, more shooting, more bullet holes, more blood, more *pow! bam! zowie!* than the moms and dads in the audience had seen in a lifetime of nightmares.

As the auditorium emptied, many parents thanked Mr. Honeycomb for calling the meeting.

"Do you think it did any good?" asked Teacher Bob.

Mr. Honeycomb shrugged. "It's a beginning," he said.

Chapter 6
The Trouble with Teamwork

The next day when Teacher Bob handed out the list of teams for the inventions project, there were cries of anger and howls of protest.

This is what Bob's list looked like:

Teams for the Invention Project

Team One: Brother/Smirk

Team Two: Bonnie/Vinnie

Team Three: Queenie/Milton

Team Four: Trudy/Skuzz

Team Five: Babs/Barry

Team Six: Harry/Gil

Team Seven: Fred/Bertha

Team Eight: Ferdy/Too-Tall

Bob had put a lot of thought into the list. While he was trying to break up cliques because of the threats and anger they caused, there was more to it than that. Bob worked hard to teach cubs language, math, history, geography, and science. But he thought it was just as important for them to learn how to work with different kinds of cubs. That was why he had insisted on naming the teams. Otherwise, it would just be more birds of a feather flocking together. In making up the teams, he had spread the members of the Too-Tall Gang among the better-behaved members of the class. His hope was that some of their good behavior would rub off on the roughneck Too-Tall Gang.

He teamed funny, pushy Queenie with Milton Chubb in hopes of getting super-shy Milton to loosen up a little. He put Babs,

who was artistic and had won prizes for her haiku, together with class comedian Barry Bruin in hopes that super-serious Babs would learn to laugh a little.

But the pairing that he was most proud of was the one that teamed Ferdy Factual with Too-Tall. The only thing that protected smug, sarcastic, super-smart Ferdy from Too-Tall's big fists was how small he was. But Ferdy's size didn't stop Too-Tall from pushing him around, hiding his books, and throwing his cap into trees. In his own way, though, Ferdy gave as good as he got. One morning when Barry was stuck for the Joke of the Day, Ferdy had offered to fill in.

"The Joke of the Day," said Ferdy. "Why is Too-Tall's IQ like the middle of winter?"

"We don't know," said the class in unison. "Why *is* Too-Tall's IQ like the middle of winter?"

"Because," said Ferdy, "they're both below zero." The class roared with laughter. Too-Tall roared with anger and chased Ferdy around the room until Teacher Bob made them sit down.

"What's the matter, Too-Tall?" asked Teacher Bob. "Can't you take a joke?"

"Sure, I can take a joke," said Too-Tall. "I just wanted to see if Nerdy Ferdy can take a punch."

Bob wasn't surprised that of all the teams he put together, the loudest protests came from Ferdy and Too-Tall.

"You can't do this to me!" cried Ferdy. "Teaming me with this brain-dead buffoon will destroy my reputation! Why, if I tried to dumb down enough to work with Too-Tall, my brain would blow a fuse!"

"Who're you calling brain-dead, you little twerp?" shouted Too-Tall. "If you don't shut

your mouth, you're gonna be *dead*-dead! And you won't have to worry about fuses, because I'm gonna put your lights out!" By now, Too-Tall was chasing Ferdy around Teacher Bob as if he were a maypole. Bob reached out and grabbed them both.

"ENOUGH!" he shouted. "I'll not have any more threats or name-calling! You two are going to find a way to work together, or I'm going to give you both zeroes on this unit! And I should warn you that this unit is going to count for a third of your mark for this report period." That stopped the threats and the name-calling. Ferdy was a straight-A student. He'd been getting straight A's since the days of blocks and fingerpainting, and he wasn't about to break the streak now. The threat worked on Too-Tall as well. His dad had told him to bring his marks up or else! Too-Tall didn't want to find out what the "or else" was.

"Okay, then," ordered Bob. "You two try to come up with an invention you can agree on." Still grumbling, the unlikely team of Ferdy and Too-Tall went off to see what they could work out. Bob's fondest hope was that in the course of working together on the inventions project, some of Ferdy's smarts would rub off on Too-Tall. It never occurred to him that it might work the other way around.

There was quite a lot of grumbling between the members of the other teams as well. Many of them were having trouble deciding which invention to choose. Babs Bruno was devoted to literature. When she suggested the printing press, class comedian Barry Bruin countered with the whoopee cushion, the hand buzzer, and itching powder.

"You're not serious!" protested Babs.

"Hey," said Barry. "What's so great about being serious?"

When they finally agreed that movies, which they both enjoyed, would be their choice, Barry said, "Fine. Let's shake on it." *Buzzzzzz* went the buzzer concealed in Barry's hand.

"YI-I-I-E-E!" screamed Babs. She was pretty angry at first, but then she laughed. After that, she and Barry got along fairly well.

Bob wanted to know how his teams were working out, so he walked around the room and listened. It wasn't going to be easy. It was all Queenie could do to loosen up super-shy Milton. But it turned out that she was a *Grapplemania* fan, too. They agreed to watch it together after school. Since they both enjoyed television, they decided that would be their invention.

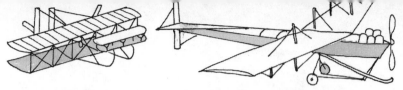

That's how it went with Brother Bear and Smirk, too. At first, it looked as if Brother and gang member Smirk wouldn't be able to agree on anything. After all, Brother was just about the only cub who stood up to the Too-Tall Gang. But once they got to know each other, they found that they had something in common: they both built model airplanes. They came up with the idea of playing the roles of the Wright Brothers and telling how they had invented the airplane. Brother would play the role of Orville, and Smirk would be Wilbear.

That's how it went with most of the teams. They had a hard time at first, but after a while they found common ground and were able to decide on an invention.

Except for Ferdy and Too-Tall.

It got so hot and heavy between them

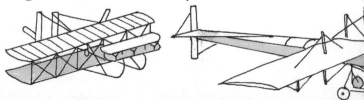

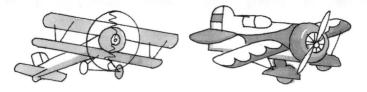

that Teacher Bob came close to interrupting a number of times. But just when Bob had decided to give up on Ferdy and Too-Tall, they had a breakthrough. At least, that's what it looked like. After a complicated hands, fists, and elbows high five, plus fanny bumps, Ferdy and Too-Tall came to Teacher Bob with big grins and two pieces of paper.

"Teacher Bob," said Ferdy, "you'll be pleased to hear that my teammate and I have finally agreed on an invention."

"Glad to hear it," said Bob. "How did you manage to agree?"

"I've been doing some reading on conflict resolution," said Ferdy. "I used one of the ideas I'd read about."

"Yeah," said Too-Tall. "I always thought conflict resolution meant a punch in the nose."

"The idea was that it's sometimes better to write things down than to shout at each other," continued Ferdy. "So that's what we did. We each made a list of five inventions. Our hope was that at least one invention would be on both lists—and it worked! One invention *was* on both lists. Here, have a look."

This is what the lists looked like:

Ferdy's List	Too-Tall's List
Radar	Firecrackers
Cyclotron	Video games
Sonar	Paintball
Electron	Flush
microscope	toilet
Guns	Guns

When Teacher Bob read the lists, his heart sank. The invention that appeared on both lists was…GUNS!

Chapter 7
Guns in the Night

Although Brother and Sister were still playing after-school shoot-'em-up games, the problem of violent after-dinner television solved itself because Brother had to work on his inventions project. Mama was still worried about the culture of violence. But what really worried Mama was guns.

"It just gives me chills to think about that Mose Moseby and his thirty-seven guns," she said.

"I have the solution to your problem with old Mose," said Papa. "We just won't invite him to afternoon tea."

"Never mind teasing me about it," said Mama.

"It's just that guns aren't going to go away, sweetie," said Papa, "and they do have their proper place."

"Proper place, indeed!" said Mama, and walked off in a huff. Papa just sighed and shrugged.

It often happens that something that's worrying you while you're awake will find its way into your dreams. That's what happened to Mama that night after she and Papa went to bed. As you might guess, what found its way into Mama's dreams was guns—big guns and small guns, guns with arms and legs, talking guns. They chased Mama all night. They chased her until some noises that went

bump in the night woke her up.

"Wha!" she said, almost waking Papa, but not quite. The noises were coming from outside. Mama went to the window and looked into the night. Papa roused himself and joined her.

"What is it, dear?" he asked.

"Prowlers," said Mama in a hushed voice. "Prowlers prowling around our garden house." Though it was dark, she could make out some figures, and...*they were wearing masks!* "Oh, dear!" said Mama. "It's a whole gang, and they're wearing robbers' masks!"

"We'll see about that!" said Papa. "I'm going down there and give them what for!"

"Don't you dare!" cried Mama, grabbing Papa's arm. "It could be dangerous! I'm going to dial 911." And she did.

"What do you suppose they're after?" asked Papa.

"I can't imagine," said Mama. "There's nothing in there except garden tools and some potatoes I'm storing.

"Shouldn't the police be here by now?" she asked after some minutes had passed. "I don't hear any sirens or see any headlights."

"The police don't use sirens on prowler calls. Sirens would scare prowlers away. And they douse their lights. The idea is to catch the prowlers."

"Shh!" hissed Mama. "I think I see a car just beyond our fence."

"And those forms sneaking up on the prowlers must be the police," hissed Papa. Suddenly, the bright light of a police flashlight shone on the masked prowlers.

"Stop in the name of the law!" shouted

Chief Bruno, with gun drawn.

"You're all under arrest!" shouted Officer Marguerite. She had a gun, too. But the masked prowlers didn't stop. They just scattered into the bushes. Nor did the chief or Marguerite shoot, because the prowlers were raccoons, who came by their robbers' masks honestly.

"Raccoons!" cried Mama. "They must have been after my potatoes."

"Come," said Papa. "We'd better get down there and apologize to the police for bringing them out on a wild goose—er, raccoon—chase."

"No need to apologize," said the chief to Mama and Papa. "It's better to be safe than sorry." The chief and Marguerite put their guns back into their holsters, went back to their car, turned on their headlights, and headed back to town.

When Mama and Papa got back upstairs, they found that the noise had wakened Brother and Sister.

"What happened?" asked Brother, rubbing his eyes.

"We'll tell you about it in the morning," said Mama. "Now back to bed with you."

"You know something?" said Mama after she and Papa were back in bed. "I have to admit that guns do have their proper place—and that place is in the hands of the police." She waited for Papa to answer, but the only answer she got was a snore.

Papa was already fast asleep.

Chapter 8
Mothers Against Violence

The next morning, after Brother and Sister were off to school and Papa was at work in his shop, Mama was reading the morning paper over a second cup of coffee. Since there had been a reporter from the *Beartown Intelligencer* at the school meeting, she wasn't too surprised to find a story about it in the paper. This is the story she saw:

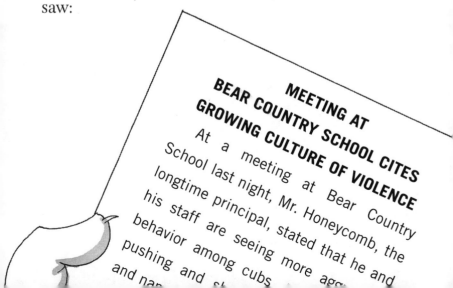

MEETING AT BEAR COUNTRY SCHOOL CITES GROWING CULTURE OF VIOLENCE

At a meeting at Bear Country School last night, Mr. Honeycomb, the longtime principal, stated that he and his staff are seeing more aggressive behavior among cubs — pushing and sh... and na...

MEETING AT
BEAR COUNTRY SCHOOL CITES
GROWING CULTURE OF VIOLENCE

At a meeting at Bear Country School last night, Mr. Honeycomb, the longtime principal, stated that he and his staff are seeing more aggressive behavior among cubs. "There's more pushing and shoving, more taunting and name-calling," said Principal Honeycomb.

When asked what he believed to be the cause, he answered without hesitation, "Violent television, movies, and video games are a big part of it."

Many of the parents present agreed. Some also raised the issue of guns. Mrs. Beverly Bruin, whose two cubs attend Bear Country School,

spoke out against guns. "I think guns are awful!" she said, adding, "I don't know why folks need to have guns."

This brought a vigorous defense of guns from Farmer Ben, whose farm is on the outskirts of Beartown—as well as an even more vigorous response from a Mr. Mose Moseby, who gave his address as "Hard by Forbidden Bog." When buttonholed after he left the meeting and asked his position on the gun issue, Mr. Moseby said, "Ain't no issue to it. But I'll tell you this: they can have my thirty-seven guns when they pry my cold, dead fingers from their barrels."

When asked what he thought of the claim that violent movies and video games were a big part of the cause of

growing violence, video store manager Steve Grizzmo said, "Stuff and non-sense. Besides, what cubs watch is their parents' responsibility, not mine."

A montage of violent television, movie, and video game footage was shown at the close of the meeting.

It was pretty scary.

Hmm, thought Mama after reading the story. The video store manager was right when he said what cubs watched was their parents' responsibility. But that wasn't the whole story. What happened to cubs was everybody's responsibility, including that video store manager's.

Mama decided then and there that it was time to stop stewing about the culture of violence and do something about it. A plan began to form in Mama's mind. She called up Mrs. Bruin and told her about it.

"That's a great plan!" said Mrs. Bruin. "Let me call some mothers, and you do the same. We'll meet for lunch at the Red Lantern."

At noon, Mama, Mrs. Bruin, and a dozen or so other mothers formed Mothers Opposed to Violent Entertainment—or MOVE, for short. Their plan was simple. The first thing they did was draw up a petition and ask the leading citizens of Bear Country to sign it. They got signatures from Dr. Gert Grizzly, head of Beartown Hospital, Judge Gavel, who interrupted a trial to sign, Chief Bruno, Officer Marguerite, and school principal Mr. Honeycomb. Their only disappointment was Mayor (Mugwump) Honeypot, who hid in his bathroom when they came to his office. Once the petition was signed, they had some special stickers printed at the Beartown Copy Center. This is what they looked like:

The mothers planned to visit the video store and ask the manager to place "Not for Cubs" stickers on his violent movies and video games. If he rejected their request...well, a lot of mothers belonged to MOVE, and they just might *move* their business to that other video store on the edge of town.

The multiplex was another problem. It had a ratings system, but young cubs were getting into movies they weren't supposed to. MOVE would speak to the multiplex manager about that.

Chapter 9
No Guns Allowed

Meanwhile, back at school, Teacher Bob's inventions unit was coming along nicely. Not only were the teams getting along, they were getting more and more excited about their presentations.

Brother and Smirk, who were building a model of Orville and Wilbear's first airplane, were planning to show how its controls worked.

Bonnie and Vinnie, who had chosen radio, were making a crystal set to demonstrate the miracle of radio.

Trudy and Skuzz, whose invention was the telegraph, had found some old telegraph keys at a flea market and planned to demonstrate Morse code.

All in all, Teacher Bob was very pleased

COMPUTER

INVENTIONS

CAMERA

by how his plan was working out. The one thing he was worried about, given all the talk about guns and the culture of violence, was Ferdy and Too-Tall's choice of invention. He decided to talk to them about it. Perhaps he could persuade them to choose another invention.

Ferdy and Too-Tall had a problem, too. But it wasn't likely to lead them to change their minds. They were, in fact, getting more and more excited about guns.

Bob called Ferdy and Too-Tall aside. "Fellows," he said, "I'm worried about your choice of guns for the inventions unit."

"Why so?" asked Ferdy.

"*Why so?*" said Bob. "Surely you've heard that there's a big fuss going on about guns and the culture of violence."

"One would have to be deaf not to have heard it," said Ferdy. "But what could that

TELESCOPE

BICYCLE

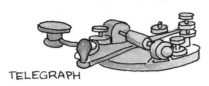
TELEGRAPH

PAPER CLIP

possibly have to do with the education process, with what we study here at school? Guns certainly pass all your study tests. There can be no question about the historical importance of guns—"

"Yes," interrupted Teacher Bob, "but you're not going to claim that guns have been a benefit to bearkind!"

"Surely you jest," said the class genius. "Guns have been an enormous benefit to bearkind. Guns were among the first products made using the idea of interchangeable parts. Why, today, everything from automobiles to toasters is made using that idea."

"That's my partner who said that," said Too-Tall with a proud grin.

Teacher Bob had to admit Ferdy was right. Besides, it wouldn't be very fair to make them change, since they'd done exactly what he had asked them to do: find

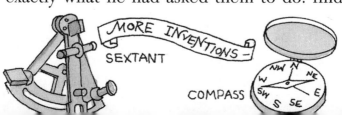
SEXTANT   MORE INVENTIONS   COMPASS

an invention they could agree on.

Bob sighed and shrugged. "Well, all right. Press on with your guns presentation."

"We certainly shall, sir," said Ferdy. "But we have a bit of a problem we'd like to discuss with you."

"Oh?" said Bob.

"No doubt you've been hearing about some of the presentations the other teams are planning. Brother and Smirk are working on a model of the Wright Brothers' first airplane. Bonnie and Vinnie will be bringing an actual crystal set to class. Trudy and Skuzz are bringing real telegraph keys to class as part of their presentation."

"Yes," said Bob, "and I'm very pleased about that."

"Then no doubt," said Ferdy, "you'll be pleased if we bring a gun to school as a part of our presentation."

Bob was aghast. "B-b-bring a gun to school?" he sputtered.

"That's right," said Too-Tall. "My dad has a rat gun. He uses it to keep down the rats in the junkyard. We'll take the bullets out, of course."

"Absolutely not!" said Bob. "Why, Mr. Honeycomb would have my head on a plate! It's absolutely out of the question."

"Is that your last word, sir?" asked Ferdy.

"It's my last word on *that* subject," said Bob, and walked away.

"I guess that shuts us down as far as bringing my dad's rat gun to school," said Too-Tall.

"Your father's rat gun is not *all* guns," said Ferdy.

"Huh?" said Too-Tall.

"We simply cannot do justice to the invention of guns without some sort of gun with which to demonstrate how its parts work together: the barrel, the stock, the trigger, the hammer, the ammunition."

"You heard Teacher Bob," said Too-Tall. "We'll both get zeroes if we go against him."

"Perhaps so," said Ferdy, "but there are more important values than high marks."

"Hey," said Too-Tall, "you're starting to sound like me."

"So be it," said Ferdy. Too-Tall was beginning to feel that he had a tiger by the tail.

Later, at recess, Too-Tall was sitting on the school steps watching Ferdy walk in circles. Round and round he went, hands clasped behind his back, head thrust forward, brow knit, deep in thought. He was thinking so hard that Too-Tall half expected smoke to come pouring out of his ears.

"Eureka!" shouted Ferdy. "I've got it!"

"Who's Eureka?" said the startled Too-Tall. "And what have you got?"

"'Eureka' is what scientists say when they solve a really pesky problem," explained Ferdy, "and what I've got is a way to get around Teacher Bob's 'no guns allowed' rule."

"What is it? Tell me!" said Too-Tall.

"Not here," said Ferdy. "We must find some place where utmost secrecy can be maintained."

"I know *just* the place," said Too-Tall.

Chapter 10
A Secret Place

"Say," said Ferdy, reading the sign atop the big truck cab that was used as an office, "isn't that your father's auto parts junkyard up ahead?"

Too-Tall didn't answer. After a while they came to a clearing behind the junkyard. At its center stood the Too-Tall Gang's secret clubhouse. It was made entirely of truck and auto parts the gang had taken from the junkyard.

"What's the purpose of all these tin cans and bells strung on these bushes?" asked Ferdy.

"Give 'em a pull and you'll find out," said Too-Tall. Ferdy pulled. The tin cans rattled, the bells jangled, and Vinnie, Smirk, and Skuzz poured out of the clubhouse, carrying chunks of wood.

"You can't bring him here, Chief!" said Skuzz.

"Shut up and get back inside," ordered Too-Tall. "We've got serious business!"

The gang looked on with amazement as, under Too-Tall's protection, Ferdy boldly marched into the clubhouse. Was this the same Nerdy Ferdy they knew from the schoolyard? Once inside, the gang sat on the car seats they'd taken from the junkyard. Too-Tall sat high on a truck seat that was sort of like a throne.

"Okay, Ferdy," said Too-Tall. "Let's hear about this gun you think we can use in our presentation without getting into big trouble. You have the floor." It was a dirt floor, so Ferdy took a stick and began to draw in the dirt.

"Since Teacher Bob has forbidden us to bring a real gun to school for purposes of demonstration," said Ferdy, "I have invented a gun that, while quite harmless, can show how guns work." The members of the gang gathered around as Ferdy began drawing his invention in the dirt. "Now, this piece of wood," said Ferdy, pointing, "will serve as both the stock and the barrel. This ordinary nail, driven halfway into the wood,

will serve as the trigger." The gang members were amazed.

"What's that little thing on the back?" asked Vinnie.

"That," explained Ferdy, "is a clothespin with a piece broken off. It serves as the gun's hammer."

"But where's the bullets?" asked Too-Tall. "What's it shoot?"

"It shoots giant rubber bands," said Ferdy, adding to the drawing.

"Hey, cool!" said Vinnie. "A giant rubber band gun!"

"But will it work?" asked Too-Tall.

"Of course it will work," said Ferdy. "All we need is a piece of board, a nail, and a clothespin. Finding giant rubber bands, however, may be a problem."

"Gang, fan out and get what Ferdy needs," ordered Too-Tall. "As for ammunition, I think I know just the place to get giant rubber bands."

"Where, pray tell?" asked Ferdy.

Too-Tall shook a thumb in the direction of his father's junkyard. "There's tons of old inner tubes there."

"How will we get them?" asked Ferdy.

"The same way we got the makings of this clubhouse. We'll sneak in and take 'em."

"I don't want to seem overly cautious," said Ferdy, "but what about your father's rat gun?"

"No problem," said Too-Tall. "My father's out of town. He's in Big Bear City buying wrecks."

"When are we going to make our little

raid?" asked Ferdy eagerly, his eyes alight with excitement. Bob's plan wasn't working out quite as expected. He had thought some of Ferdy's smarts would rub off on Too-Tall. But that was not what was happening. Instead of Too-Tall becoming a little smarter, Ferdy was slowly turning into Mr. Macho.

"Twilight's the best time," said Too-Tall. "It'll be dark enough so we won't be seen and light enough for us to find our way around."

Soon after, Smirk, Vinnie, and Skuzz returned with enough lengths of board, nails, and clothespins to build enough giant rubber band guns for a small army.

Chapter 11
The Raid

So while the mothers and most of the leading citizens of Beartown were working to slow down the growing culture of violence, a shadowy group was setting out to get ammunition for Ferdy's invention: the giant rubber band gun. And though it was hard to see in the twilight, it appeared that the shadowy figure in the lead was none other than Ferdy Factual.

"Hey, wait up!" hissed Too-Tall. "*I'm* the leader of this pack." Ignoring him, Ferdy found a place where the junkyard's fence was loose at the bottom and pulled it up.

"Here," he ordered Too-Tall. "Hold this up so that the rest of us can get through."

Too-Tall was so surprised at being ordered around that he did what he was told. Keeping low, the raiders threaded through the spooky junkyard in search of an old inner tube. But at the very moment they found a pile of them, something scary happened.

Lights went on in the truck cab office, and there, big as life and twice as frightening, was Too-Tall's dad, back early from his trip to Big Bear City. He must have heard something, because he was reaching for his big black rat gun.

"Run," hissed Too-Tall in a panic. "He thinks we're rats!"

"Freeze!" ordered Ferdy. "Get down behind these tires and *don't move!*"

BLAM went the rat gun. It was the loud-est *blam* any of them had ever heard. Smirk, Vinnie, and Skuzz were shaking like leaves. Too-Tall was shaking like a bowlful of jelly in an earthquake. The only raider who remained calm, cool, and collected was Ferdy.

"What'll we *doooo?*" wailed Too-Tall.

"We will remain absolutely quiet and perfectly still until dark," ordered Ferdy. "Then we'll choose a good, stretchy inner tube and make our exit. Is that understood?"

"Y-y-y-yes," blithered Too-Tall. The gang members looked at Too-Tall as if they hardly knew him.

It was dark when they got back to the clubhouse. The gang turned on the lights, and Ferdy went to work on his giant rubber band gun.

The gang watched admiringly as he worked. First he cut the inner tube into big rubber bands. Then he put all the parts together.

"Hmm," said Ferdy as he loaded the gun. "I think it just might be possible to make a *repeating* rubber band gun.

"Okay," he said when he was ready to fire. "What should I hit?"

"How about that horn?" said Vinnie, pointing to an old-fashioned horn attached to the wall. *Zip* went the rubber band. *HONK* went the horn.

"Hey, cool!", "Terrific!", "Way to go!" said the gang members as they gathered around Ferdy, slapping him on the back. All except Too-Tall, who just sat in the corner and stared.

"Losing face" is an expression that means losing the respect of others. But Too-Tall didn't just lose face, he lost what for him was the most precious thing in the world: his reputation as the toughest, baddest, most fearless cub around. Even as he sat there staring, he was trying to think of some way of getting his lost reputation back.

Chapter 12
Showdown!

It was the day all the teams had been working toward: presentation day in Teacher Bob's class. The teams all were ready to present their inventions, complete with speeches, drawings, and live demonstrations. The different teams were trying to keep their presentations under wraps. Brother and Smirk had their model of the Wright Brothers' first plane in a box. Bonnie and Vinnie had their crystal set wrapped in tissue paper. Trudy and Skuzz were keeping their telegraph keys in a pizza box.

Ferdy tried to keep to himself when he arrived in the schoolyard. But the members of the class couldn't help but notice that he was carrying a large object under his arm. It was concealed beneath a raincoat.

The teams would be presenting their inventions over the next couple of days. Teacher Bob had set today as the deadline so that none of the teams would have extra preparation time. Though there was an air of excitement among the members of Bob's class, none of them had any idea what wild, mad, *dangerous* excitement would be taking place in the schoolyard within a very few minutes.

Too-Tall had lain awake all night brooding about how he had turned into a shivering, shaking bowlful of jelly—and how Ferdy had kept his cool. He remembered how the gang had looked at him—and how

they had looked at Ferdy. It was all Ferdy's fault. It was Ferdy who had caused him to lose face. He had to do something about Ferdy: wipe him out, destroy him, reduce him to a puddle. If he didn't, he would lose his position as the feared head of the notorious Too-Tall Gang. A plan was beginning to form in Too-Tall's troubled mind.

It was almost time to line up for the morning bell. Someone noted that Too-Tall hadn't arrived yet. Someone else suggested that he might be playing hooky. But that didn't seem likely. The Too-Tall Gang usually played hooky together, and the rest of the gang was already at school.

Wait! There he was now! But what was that he was carrying? It couldn't possibly be what it looked like. There was no way that even Too-Tall would bring a gun to school. But that's what it was—a big, black, dangerous-looking gun! A cry went up. "He's got a gun! He's got a gun!" The students of Bear Country School scattered every which way.

Gun at the ready, Too-Tall marched through the schoolyard in search of Ferdy. By now, panic had spread throughout the yard. But one cub kept her head. As you might expect, it was Babs Bruno, the police chief's daughter. She ran to the schoolyard pay phone, popped in a coin, and called her father's direct number. When he came on the phone, she said in a firm, clear voice, "It's an emergency, Dad! Too-Tall's got a gun, and we think he's after Ferdy!"

"We're on our way!" shouted the chief.

Meanwhile, Too-Tall spotted Ferdy on the far side of the schoolyard. Everybody looked on in horror. They froze when Too-Tall shouted, "There you are, you double-crossing little creep," and moved within shooting distance of Ferdy. It was like those action scenes in the movies when everything goes into slow motion. Too-Tall slowly raised his gun and aimed it at Ferdy. But when he pulled the trigger, *there was no bang!* There was no sound at all, except the wet hiss of a powerful stream of water. Because Too-Tall's big, black, dangerous-looking gun wasn't a real gun at all—it was a Powersoaker!

It certainly soaked Ferdy. The stream of water soaked him from head to toe. Too-Tall howled with laughter. Smirk, Vinnie, and Skuzz howled with laughter. Everybody howled with laughter.

Everybody, that is, except Ferdy. Ferdy calmly whipped the raincoat off the object he was carrying under his arm. It was a giant *repeating* rubber band gun. When Too-Tall saw it, his laughter turned to fear. He turned and ran, but not fast enough to

outrun those big stinging rubber bands.

"Yow!…Yow!…Yow!" yelled Too-Tall as he ran across the schoolyard. But Too-Tall's shouts were lost in the scream of sirens as three police cars and a SWAT truck roared into the schoolyard.

"Drop that gun, Too-Tall!" ordered the chief as the SWAT team poured out of the truck, carrying real guns.

"It's just a water gun!" cried Too-Tall, dropping it.

"And you drop that…whatever that thing is, Ferdy!" said the chief. Ferdy dropped his rubber band gun.

By now the entire faculty, including Principal Honeycomb, was in the school-yard. There was great confusion and cries of "What happened? What happened?" as everyone crowded around.

"Stand back!" ordered Chief Bruno as the helmeted SWAT team stood by, guns at the ready. The chief picked up Too-Tall's Powersoaker. "Hmm," he said, examining it closely. "It looks like a real gun, right down to the last detail. We're going to keep this." He handed it to Officer Marguerite. "Young fellow," he said to Too-Tall, "you just had a close call. My officers had no way of knowing it wasn't a real gun. Now, who owns this thing?" asked the chief, picking up the rubber band gun.

"I do, sir," said Ferdy. "I invented it myself."

"I'd say it's more like you *re*-invented it," said the chief. "We made guns like this when we were cubs. Mr. Honeycomb," he said, turning to the principal, "I'm sure there's a story behind this mess, but I don't want to hear it. I just want to say this, and I want you all to remember it. When guns get into the wrong hands—any kind of guns, even toy guns—things have a way of getting *out* of hand. Now, I don't want to hear about guns at Bear Country School ever again. Is that understood?"

Mr. Honeycomb nodded.

The faculty nodded.

The students nodded.

Ferdy and Too-Tall nodded especially hard.

It would be a day that was long remem-

bered at Bear Country School. Many ideas were bumping up against each other in Teacher Bob's mind as he led his students into the school. No doubt Mr. Honeycomb would be calling another teachers' meeting on the subject of the culture of violence. And perhaps Miss Glitch would once again suggest removing all violent literature from the library. And perhaps Mr. Grizzmeyer would once again suggest that the school grounds be declared off-limits for all threats, taunts, and name-calling. And perhaps those ideas should be considered. But Bob had a class to teach—so, for the moment, it would have to be first things first. And the first thing he had to do was get Ferdy out of those wet clothes. Then they could get on with the invention presentations.

Chapter 13
A Quiet Supper at Home

It was the evening of the day of what came to be known as the "Gunfight at Bear Country School." Brother and Sister, who had been in the "eye of the storm," were still a little shaken up when the family sat down to supper.

"Well," said Papa, "you had quite a time for yourselves at school today."

"I guess so," said Brother.

"It's all over the television and the news-papers," continued Papa. "They were even talking about it down at the general store."

"Now, Papa," said Mama, "I'm not sure this is something we need to talk about at supper. I don't want the cubs upset."

"Perhaps," said Papa. "But it looks like they're *already* upset."

"It was scary," said Sister, staring at her soup.

"What was so scary about it?" asked Papa. "I understand that it was just a toy gun."

"Yes. But it looked so real!" said Sister. "And Too-Tall looked so angry. It was *really* scary when he aimed it at Ferdy."

"But of course, it wasn't a real gun. It was a Powersoaker," said Brother, "and all Ferdy got was wet."

"What happened then?" asked Papa.

"Everybody laughed," said Brother. "It

seemed real funny at the time."

"But not anymore?" commented Papa.

"I guess not," said Brother. "Things got serious real fast when the police arrived."

"It was pretty scary," said Sister.

"I spent all afternoon simmering this soup," Mama said. "Will you please eat it before it gets cold?" The members of the Bear family ate soup for a while.

"I'm sure it was all very exciting and scary," said Papa as Mama served the honey-cured salmon and sweet potatoes. "But did you learn anything from today's experience? Mmm! These sweet potatoes are delicious, my dear."

"Yes," said Sister. "I learned that guns are bad and dangerous!"

"Are they *always* bad and dangerous?" asked Papa.

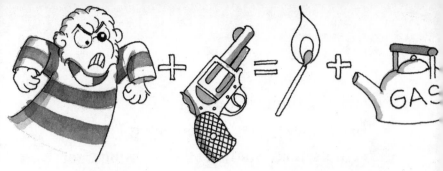

"That's a good question," said Brother. "After all, Gramps has guns. He uses them for target practice. It's one of his hobbies. But he keepsh 'em locked up in a casch."

"Please don't speak with your mouth full," said Mama.

"Okay, then," said Papa. "Let me ask you this: *When* are guns dangerous?"

"They're dangerous when bad guys get them!" said Sister.

"Is Too-Tall a bad guy?" asked Papa.

"He can be," said Brother. "But that wasn't the problem today. The problem today was that he was very, very angry!"

"I think you've got it!" said Papa. "It's *anger* that makes guns dangerous. Anger to a gun is like a lit match to gasoline: when they're put together, bad things can happen."

"Well," said Sister, "I agree with Mama. I think guns are bad, bad, bad, and they should be wiped off the face of the earth. And I, for one, am not going to play any more gun games!"

"That's okay with me," said Brother. "I think we're sort of outgrowing them anyway. Mama, may I have some more salmon?"

"My position on guns isn't *quite* that extreme," explained Mama, passing the salmon. "I think the police certainly need them. But I'm delighted to hear that you're outgrowing gun games—and I'm thinking that maybe, just maybe, you're outgrowing all those awful violent television shows and video games."

"But television and video games are different from guns!" protested Brother.

"How are they different?" asked Mama.

"That's easy!" said Brother. "Guns can hurt you. But television and video games never hurt anybody."

"I'm not sure I agree with that!" said Mama. "Certainly, guns in the wrong hands can do bad things. But violent television and video games can do bad things, too: they can make you think that violence is just an everyday thing—and I don't like the idea of folks getting used to shooting and killing, even if it is just pretend."

"Well said, my dear," said Papa. He had picked up the TV schedule and was looking at it. He saw that his favorite show was about to come on. "Hey!" he said. "I've got a great idea! After all this heavy discussion, I think we're entitled to have our dessert in

front of the television—and it just so happens that my favorite show is on."

"Oh," said Mama, "what show is that?"

"*Cartoon Theater*, featuring Cunning Coyote and the Birdrunner."

"Cunning Coyote and the Birdrunner?" exclaimed Mama. "Why, that's the most violent show of all."

"But, my dear," said Papa, scratching his head, "Cunning Coyote isn't violent, it's funny."

Mama sighed. She brought the dessert and joined the family in front of the television. She couldn't help giggling as she watched Cunning Coyote try to smash Birdrunner with a rock, blow him up with a big firecracker, and hit him over the head with a giant hammer. As she watched Cunning Coyote and Birdrunner go through their paces, she realized that while the culture of violence was a big and important problem, it wasn't going to be a simple one to solve.

Stan and Jan Berenstain began writing and illustrating books for children in the early 1960s, when their two young sons were beginning to read. That marked the start of the best-selling Berenstain Bears series. Now, with more than one hundred books in print, videos, television shows, and even Berenstain Bears attractions at major amusement parks, it's hard to tell where the Bears end and the Berenstains begin!

Stan and Jan make their home in Bucks County, Pennsylvania, near their sons—Leo, a writer, and Michael, an illustrator—who are helping them with Big Chapter Books stories and pictures. They plan on writing and illustrating many more books for children, especially for their four grandchildren, who keep them well in touch with the kids of today.